"In the plainspoken language of a trustwo... *Spring Hallelujah* is an extended hand and in... ...ut and into a place of careful thought and purpose. On this oft-wilded path, every verse is a warm and appreciative inquiry into considering and reconsidering the complexities of life's pain and joy and a cultivation of patience for the liminal spaces in between. If compassionate empathy is the highest, most human state of consciousness, this collection will be a Springtime of it, quickening a hopeful sense of all that is waiting for you after all and in every season."

–JAMES SCOTT SMITH, Author of *Water, Rocks and Trees*

"Heidi Barr's *Cold Spring Hallelujah* isn't so much a series of poetic meditations as it is a love letter to slowing down and taking notice of the healing gifts in the world around us. In a culture that seems so focused on the epic, on the larger than life, of 'go big or go home,' Barr suggests a different path. 'Let's do something different,' she urges, 'and accept the mundane.' The gorgeous poems she shares as gentle suggestions in how we might do so make me grateful for her company in the trying."

–CHRIS LA TRAY, award winning author of *One-Sentence Journal*

"*Cold Spring Hallelujah* changed my pace and found the forest of my soul where all things are connected. As I read, I am pulled into the seasons and moments between them, where ordinary details are reclaimed as holy delight. I am glad for the reminder to consider God with reverent wonder and nature as a worthy neighbor."

–PASTOR META HERRICK CARLSON, author of *Ordinary Blessings*

"In this high velocity age of soul-blinding techno-digital distraction, material accumulation, and spiritual grasping, Heidi Barr's *Cold Spring Hallelujah* is a breath of fresh air. This gentle, flowing collection is an antidote to the impoverished consciousness of these maddening times. Barr's poems demonstrate how to slow down and come into holy union with the numinous that is ever-present in our everyday lives."

–FRANK LARUE OWEN, poet, author of *The School of Soft-Attention*

"We all know that feeling of a cold spring; usually, we want it to be otherwise. But in these poems of triumph and authentic awareness, Heidi Barr gifts us with lines that sparkle, that remind us to stay open and welcoming when resistance and torment are uppermost in our thoughts. Be enamored with your existence, she writes. A powerful message that nourishes the soul, and just like the warmth of hot tea when chilled to the bone, Barr's collection has a magnetic quality you'll want to experience time and time again. A book for lingering."

—D.A. HICKMAN, author of *Ancients of the Earth: Poems of Time*

"In an age when it can be challenging to identify beauty amongst sadness, the injustice and the messy unfolding, *Cold Spring Hallelujah* offers something other than simple hope or optimism. Heidi Barr offers an invitation to trust what is on the other side of each moment. It is an anthem for the inevitable turns of death & rebirth in this life—an expression of thanksgiving and rejoice from the deepest—and at times—darkest, recesses of our being. It's bound to become one of those works that gets passed along, like a family prayer or favorite story that always arrives exactly when and where it is needed most. Keep these poems close to your arm chair—I expect they will be the kind of company you will want to welcome, even on the quietest of days."

—LINDSEY RUDER, writer, farmer, yogi and wellness seeker

"Heidi's words always go straight to the heart. This beautiful book of poems allows you to put your thoughts on hold for a minute and reconnect you with the earth's energy. She writes about the beauty of nature, the need to explore and the magic that you can find in between the seasons. These words are a portal to what has almost been lost, our connection to source."

—IRIS SUURLAND, Founder of the Nabalo Company

COLD SPRING HALLELUJAH

COLD SPRING *HALLELUJAH*

POETRY BY

HEIDI BARR

Homebound Publications
Ensuring that the mainstream isn't the only stream.

HOMEBOUND PUBLICATIONS

Ensuring the mainstream isn't the only stream

Postal Box 1442, Pawcatuck, Connecticut 06379-1442

WWW.HOMEBOUNDPUBLICATIONS.COM

© 2019 • Text by HEIDI BARR

First published in the United States of America
by Homebound Publications 2019.

Quantity sales. Special discounts are available on quantity purchases
by corporations, associations, bookstores and others. For details, contact
the publisher or visit wholesalers such as Ingram or Baker & Taylor.

HARDCOVER ISBN • 978-1-947003-56-9
PAPERBACK ISBN • 978-1-938846-85-4
Front Cover Image © Brian Bradley
Interior Images
Ferns © Nikita Tikhomirov
Stone Path © Ashim D'Silva
Suspension Bridge © Nico E.

Cover and Interior Designed by Leslie M. Browning

Printed in the United States of America
10 9 8 7 6 5 4 3 2 1

Homebound Publications is committed to ecological stewardship.
We greatly value the natural environment and invest in environmental conservation.

TABLE OF CONTENTS

CONFESSION

FORGIVENESS

COMMUNION

BENEDICTION

For those who seek healing.
_____

And even though it all went wrong
I'll stand before the lord of song
With nothing on my tongue but hallelujah
—Leonard Cohen

INTRODUCTION

THIS COLLECTION OF POEMS CAME INTO BEING one cold spring, at what would be the close of a long struggle with persistent illness—not the sort of illness that leaves you bedridden or enduring invasive treatments, just the kind that leaves you cranky, lethargic, and wondering if this is just how it's going to be from now on. I would start to feel better and then another round of fatigue and coughing or some other infection or allergy would invade and the cycle would start all over again. It felt like I had too many things to manage, things were too hard, there were too many projects and work commitments and responsibilities—and not enough energy for it all. I wanted to be living a life rooted in simplicity, and I was tired of not feeling like myself. So I started writing one poem a day in a journal—just the things that were on my mind—no perfecting, no agonizing over the quality, just jotting down whatever words came through the pen that particular day. Poems were the right length, and their simplicity and brevity seemed like something my life at the time needed. Thoughts about self acceptance to seedlings to social media to hiking to God (and everything in between) were swirling around, and focusing on the words that found their way onto paper was one way of processing what felt like a constant, albeit muted, struggle. I wanted to claim the story that was mine, whatever that turned out to be, even if it wasn't what I would have chosen in an ideal world. Short arrangements of words seemed to somehow help with doing that.

You could say we are all broken, but then again, you could say we are all part of a collective hallelujah, and that might be closer to the truth. The world is made of stories, which are made of words, or just ideas, spoken or not, and all stories can be interpreted and told differently. It depends on the lenses through which the world is viewed and the languages spoken and heard. But no matter what stories we find ourselves in and no matter how we interact with the multitudes that constantly swirl around us, everyone can benefit from an invitation to claim truth.

So, an invitation, if I may be so bold:

> Claim the stories that invite peace. Claim the stories that create a more beautiful world, whatever beauty looks and feels like to you right now. Claim the right to choose the things that call instead of the things that beckon or taunt. Claim the clarity that listening to the deep and still parts of yourself can offer. Claim the stories that originate in your soul, the stories that bind you to the earth as part of one universal body. Claim the stories that proclaim your (sometimes fractured) human radiance in ways that the wind and the rain and the morning sun can understand.

This is certainly not a simple invitation to accept: Claiming is not an easy task, just like telling a true story can be the most challenging feat of a lifetime. But acknowledging and giving voice to the story that wants to be claimed is the first step—something that has to happen to shore up the foundation for a beautiful way of being in the world.

I've been drawn to these words of Dr. Clarissa Pinkola Estes ever since I read them years ago: She writes, "If you have a deep scar, that is a door, if you have an old, old story, that is a door. If you love the sky and the water so much you almost cannot bear it, that is a door. If you yearn for a deeper life, a full life, a sane life, that is a door." We all have a door into the story which is ours to embody and proclaim. It may be broken, or off its hinges, or hidden behind weeds, but it's there and worthy of a hallelujah.

Invocation

UNDECIDED

This nameless time
between seasons
seems to defy designation.

Winter? Spring?
It's undecided,
or simply uninterested in being labeled.

The skeleton trees,
standing watch over lingering snow
whisper, wait

as tiny moss spores
yawn, unfurl,
  astonished
    they remember
    the sun.

MELT

There's a day after winter
but before spring
when the stream
behind the house runs.

One year it ran in February,
and we didn't know what to do.

But usually it runs in March,
letting us know
spring wants in
on the composition.

It sings through cascades and ripples, a
choir of rocks and sticks and swirling mud.

Turns out,
winter and spring
together make
beautiful music.

EQUINOX

It's the time
when light
and dark
are balanced

and the sky
is open
to new
ways of being

and people
are open
to new
ways of seeing

even when
balance shifts
the very next day
and we begin again.

FREEDOM

We put on mud boots
and walk down to the lake
where the sun encourages
spring melt to go.

So we go, too,
and I forget my phone.

You poke at ice,
intent on making
a clear path
for the water,
wholly absorbed in your task.

I try to find that
quality of attention
in myself
but end up thinking,
"maybe I'll take a picture."

But I can't—
because, you know,
I forgot my phone.

After awhile,
we pick our way
back to the house
to thaw cold toes and fingers.

Back inside, I don't pick up the phone
because there is nothing to post,
and somehow
I feel freer
than I have in awhile.

COLD CLEAN AIR

Contentment means
being present
in all the ways
being present
is possible;

Moving through
a snowy forest,
tromping with a child
around a blindingly white lake,
following deer paths
along icy ridges.

Inhaling cold clean air,
holding it close while
anticipating the scent
of cedar logs burning brightly.

Just to name a few.

These things
are what is real
and what matters,

even though that sly one
who goes by virtual validation
would have you believe otherwise.

EMERGING

A bear wakes up
in spring
to get back to the business
of living out loud,
    breathing fresh air
        moving though
days with intention.

Maybe a person
in spring
can do the same—
get back to the business
of living out loud,
    breathing fresh air
        moving through
days with intention.

We creatures
are not so different
from one another
if we pay attention
    to the things of living
        reminding us what
it means to thrive.

THE BACKWOODS

How could it be I awoke, one
late spring morning, full of despair,
longing for anything different, ready
to give up on happiness, acquiesce to pain,
when something told me to stop off at the trail
leading toward the back woods, the forest home
to a birch stand, some stately oaks and multitudes
of migrating winged guests.

So I did, and those trees and birds,
together with lingering snow and
commanding spring sun firmly reminded me
nothing is permanent;
Transformation is always afoot,
and is,
in fact,
Happening this very moment.

SPRING BLIZZARD

There are a few options
when snow keeps falling
well after you wish it would stop.

You can curse the weather man, and
let a fine film of melancholy
coat your perception of life,

or

you can set out into the great white unknown,
perhaps on skis if you're feeling adventurous,
chuckling along with Old Man Winter

as he reminds you that
his mother, Nature,
always gets the last word.

INVINCIBLE SUMMER

The year it snowed
three feet in April
we had to dig
pretty deep
to find the
invincible summer
people like
to talk about;
but eventually we
did find it, and it
happened when we
laid down on the
towering snow banks
and they began to
melt as heat
from our bodies
turned them into
pools of liquid light.

SHOWING UP

I always look forward to
when the Bloodroot blooms-
it never shows up quite
where I think it will,
but it always comes back,
startling me with
its ability to persist and
make its own decisions
on where to root
and be seen.

AWAKENING

There's a day in spring
when fairies emerge
from wherever they go
in the depths of winter—

a day when lichen reaches
just a bit higher to meet the sun,
and moss puts out a
vibrant green welcome mat,

when wild creatures everywhere,
those who sing, crawl, slither, or lumber;
and yes, even those who speak;
meet in that place Rumi named,

the one between wrongdoing
and rightdoing, because that's
where tired stories give way
as awakening overtakes the earth.

BELONGING

Just like maples
unfurling their leaves
seem to hum
with a deep confidence
about where they belong,
know that you, too,
can find a home
in that wild family of things.

In memory of poet Mary Oliver,

September 10, 1935 – January 17, 2019

THAT DAY

Then one day
it was time to blossom,
and the sky welcomed
such courage with arms
that made you sigh
in expansion and reach
toward the setting sun
with the sort of gratitude
that coats the land
with goodness
and grace.

WHAT JOY IS

Joy is a tiny purple flower
emerging from ground
that seems too cold to give life.

Joy is a raindrop
meandering down your face
when drought breaks.

Joy is a feather
found tucked in a hollow tree,
reminding you some neighbors don't talk, they sing.

Joy is noticing
undulations of life
unfolding all around.

SHATTERED

A wise young man
once said, it is finished,
and the sky turned black.
They say the curtain of heaven
was torn in two that day, and I
wonder what the curtain looks like now,
after what was broken became new; when
what became new so often still seems broken.
When will we realize that what we really need
is a different sort of beginning than the kind
we are used to? One that's a bit more
like a ceramic bowl, shattered,
then pieced back together
one shard at a time,
one act of love
at a time
in a mosaic
of broken
beauty.

HERE COMES THE SUN

It's Easter morning
and even though
the first thing I did
this year was ski
through a blanket
of freshly fallen snow,
and spring seems light-years away,
there is new life
emerging along with the day,
and the older I get
the more I'm convinced
the Son and the sun
are parts of one universal whole,
and try as we might
we'll never truly know
what God is
or was
or could be;
we can only love,
each day
in the light
that we have,
rising when we must
and trusting
questioning
living
what will forever
remain a mystery.

WALKING ON WATER

One morning this past winter
the fox that claimed ownership
of the south facing hill
trotted to the middle of the lake.

The ice looked more
like a tranquil pool,
reflecting and shimmering,
a fine film of water
glossing the surface, and

suddenly she was ethereal,
floating over water,
announcing
perhaps Jesus
has come back,
and does again and again,
it's just that God wants
to experience life
in the bodies of all things,
from fox
to child
to pine bough
to centipede.

Who am I to say
a fox can't
walk on water?

THE GOD I KNOW

The God I know
has lots of sons
and daughters
and those who don't
identify with either of those labels.

The God I know
walks the streets
and carries water;
sits with those who
know nothing but pain.

The God I know
is the bedrock of the land,
the crash of the ocean
and forgotten paths
up the back of the mountain.

The God I know
loves without borders
and seeps into parts
of the world that seem devoid of light,

carrying a whisper of something
we may never understand
in a language we knew
before we were born.

CONFESSION

BROKEN

It is easy to forget
we are whole already
despite brokenness
and imperfection.

Those imperfections create holes
and those holes are wells for goodness
        and love
                and acceptance; for
beauty residing in shadows
when we don't try to blind it
with too much light.

Perhaps we need those holes
to be whole,
after all.

SUFFERING

Maybe it's futile
to look for meaning
when what I need
is strength instead.

LIFE'S WORK

Can we find truth
in the broken beauty
of an earthly experience?

What does the darkness
before dawn
have to say about
what it means to be peace?

Where is the healing
for a crushed blossom
or an unripe fruit
that falls off the vine?

When does being uncomfortable
teach us something
and when it is something
that needs to stop?

How do we live well
amidst
more questions
than answers?

UNRAVEL

I take
to walking
outside
even when
all I can think is
"I don't want to,"

drinking in
fresh air and
muted sunlight,
an act declaring
the start
of something

unraveling; an
unbecoming
powerful
enough
to change
my mind.

THINGS OF INTEREST

It's easy
to beat yourself up

over the little things.

What if instead
you said
oh, that's interesting;

and got curious
instead of angry?

Gratitude
and grace
for self
(and others).

JOURNEY

They say a journey
of a thousand miles
begins with a single step.

Or maybe every step
is a journey,
one where there is no arriving,

just the journey
and being present for it
(whatever that means).

UNSOLICITED ADVICE

Don't say you're sorry
when you could say thank you.

Gratitude often has
more power than guilt.

HAPPINESS IS A CLOUD

Happiness.
It comes and goes.

It can't be caught, or
made to cooperate.

It's not something you can pay for
and keep on your shelf.

It's more like a fine mist,
one that floats over a woodland lake.

Happiness is a cloud.
It comes and goes.

EVERYTHING HAPPENS

"Everything happens for a reason"
is a phrase I'd like to set on the curb
to be picked up by someone else.

Or maybe, better yet,
to place in a glowing wood stove
where it can turn from platitude to ash.

It's true that everything happens,
but maybe there is no reason
we need to find.

Perhaps we should just say
"Everything happens"
and leave it at that.

GO TO THE EDGES

Go to the edges of your skin,
but don't try to step
into someone else's.

Take up space
in a way that feels right and good.
Don't apologize for it.

Be in your body.

Let it be your gateway
to pleasure and adventure,
everything in between.

Surrender to contrast
that makes you shiver with delight.

Own your edges,
visit them often, and remember

the best place to be is
somewhere in the tension
between want and need.

Learning to be there allows
you to take up the space
you are meant to embody.

A FEW QUESTIONS

Could you stop to notice
the beauty of a pebble in the rain;
hear the gentle rustle of leaves
when the wind changes direction;
feel the warmth of the sun
after the fog lifts?

Could you look into eyes
belonging to the other—
maybe even someone
who seems completely opposite,
and see truth reflected back?

Could you accept yourself
as whole and complete, and
let that acceptance tell
a story you haven't yet heard,
one full of beauty?

Could you ask
"What is it like to be you?"
of a stranger
and of yourself?

What would change if you could?

LITTLE BITS OF GOOD

Maybe it's crazy, but
let's do something different and
accept the mundane.

Sit with sadness.
Go outside even though it's cold
or hot or windy or some other imperfection.

Look the cashier in the eye.
Notice the flash of a bird's wings in flight.
Put the television in the basement closet.

Grow some kale.
Be among wildflowers.
Feel cool rain on bare skin.

Those little bits of good,
combined,
might just change your world.

WHERE THE MAGIC HAPPENS

Embracing uncertainty
and failure
and mess
lets a bit of the mystery
back in.

Real change comes
when you
and me
and all of us
figure out what we stand for
and stand for it,
no matter what.

That's where
the magic
happens.

REPLACE POSITIVE THINKING WITH REALITY

I say
feel what you feel,
even if it doesn't include
sunshine and roses and kittens.

Honor what's going on,
not by sinking into despair,
but by observing
and feeling
whatever it is
you need to without
attaching a label.

Because then the
unwanted stuff
doesn't claim
(quite as much)
power.

Maybe uncertainty
 (or even failure)
is the best outcome
if it allows living
fully in the present,
owning what matters, and
setting aside what doesn't.

That might just offer
the opportunity
to shift perspective
or forgive
or build resiliency—

which sounds like
the kind of reality
I'd like to inhabit.

TENSION

Some days I want
life to feel easy,
like everything I want
is being handed to me
on that elusive silver platter.

Some days I need
to feel challenged and inspired,
like everything I require
is just far enough away
to require a bit of hard work to get there.

Some days what I want
and what I need
are in alignment
and some days they're not.

So I think, then, the best place to be
is somewhere in the gray,
tip-toeing the line
that defines desire.

WORRY VS. LAMENT

We would all do well
to let go of anxiety
as a lifestyle.

The present is more appealing
when it's not being
crowded out by a fight

between past and future
to see who can cause
the most trouble.

DEVOTION

We are devoted to
what we give attention,
so what if we gave attention
to the sacred found in stones,
seas, and clouds,
along with everything else
wild, outside ourselves
and within?

ORDINARY COURAGE

It's the stuff
that doesn't make headlines,
like when you tell your one
true story and it's the
scariest thing you've ever done,
but it's also the thing
that makes you brave, and
somehow a warrior emerges
from the depths,
one who can summon victory
from the everyday strife of life,
slaying the demons who
ride alongside fear
by reminding the world
that love always wins.

PRIVILEGE

One definition of privilege
is to opt out of thinking
about something
because you can.

It's a very real
phenomenon,
one that must be
considered constantly.

A story built on
broken systems
is hard to hear
if you make yourself
listen to the whole thing.

And if that
makes you
uncomfortable
now's the time to
start paying attention.

We have to listen to all the chapters
and peer through all the lenses
to do all the hard work if
we want to move closer
to a more beautiful
world.

MOUNTAIN SHADOW

What would it take
for humans to live
on earth in a way
that recognizes
frogs,
    boulders, and
        lichen
as neighbors instead of "nature"?

We can pass
all the laws we want
but until we learn
to live outside what 'Mother Culture'
harolds as correct,

——

Us vs. Them
More
Better
Faster

——

we'll be stuck wondering
what it would be like
to recognize ourselves
in the shadow
of the mountain,

instead of knowing
without a doubt
that we have a place in
this wild and wonderful
body of earth.

THE GOD I KNOW, PART TWO

The God I know
walks across borders,
children in hand,
because it's the only thing
left to do.

The God I know
rocks toddlers
who shiver in fear
because what they know
feels gone forever.

The God I know
walks with parents
who wonder what they could have done
while worry sits, silent and heavy
on their shoulders.

The God I know
whispers in the ears
of those who wonder about following orders
from others who are afraid
of what it means to love your neighbor.

The God I know
loves without limits
and weeps into the parts

of the world that seem far too broken—
that God wants us to remember

there is no such thing
as other people's children
and we belong to each other,
just like the source of all things
belongs to all, unwavering even today.

FORGIVENESS

PROMISE

Morning holds
a promise for day
that says even if things
get really hard,
I'll be here again
tomorrow.

THREE BROKEN HALLELUJAHS

The first came
when you realized
life had to be lived
from attention,
not distraction
which meant slowing down
enough to notice
the way soil
smells after rain.

The second came
when you detected
the elegant whisper
of a fern uncurling
the spring after wildfire
burned your beloved
forest to the ground.

The third came
when you witnessed
a convict in orange
lifting soft eyes
to a sky suddenly filled
with a murmuration of birds
singing like a thousand
hallelujahs.

THE PLACE TO SEND YOUR PRAYERS

It is a thin place,
that place between
knowledge and myth.

It is found in snow falling
on silent water and
the first bits of green
poking through last year's faded glory.

It is found in the startling
sweet taste of a wild blueberry and
the cry of a loon
through darkness.

It is found in a dying
man's last breath and
his partner's grief and gratitude
as they weave together in holy silence.

It is found in a mother's head
turning toward the sunrise
after a sleepless night and
the ecstatic cry of a child's delight.

The place to send your prayers
might seem thin—
but then again,
prayers can fit anywhere.

PHOENIX

When the door slams
may its reverberations
create just enough opening
for potential,
joy,
and love
as the old
startles the new
into being.

May we use the closing
—no matter how harsh—
to create space
for the thoughts,
the energy,
the experiences
that invite things
like potential,
like joy,
like love
into being.

May one version
of what is enough
for a beautiful life,
rise from embers left
in the ashes of old.

May what rises be enough;
let us see the grace in that.

UNNOTICED GRATITUDE

You might say you are thankful
for good health, family, friends, and food,
if you are fortunate enough to have those things.

Maybe you are thankful for a good job,
a nice car,
a successful quarter,
a negative test result.

But what goes unnoticed,
even for those who are veterans
at practicing gratitude?

Maybe it's the feel
of a warm oak-plank floor
as the wood stove gets going
late in the evening.

Maybe it's the contrast
a chaotic barn provides
to the unusually tidy house
when you go feed the chickens
before guests arrive.

Maybe it's the gasp of frigid air
into your lungs,
piercing your attention,

reminding you how
extraordinary
it is to experience life
on a living Earth
that is constantly in flux
and always changing.

Maybe it's a vivid red
cardinal
against a backdrop
of alabaster,
framed by the boughs
of a tired evergreen.

Maybe it's the way
late afternoon light
filters through ice crystals
clinging to hay
left in the fields.

Maybe it's a heart that beats,
even if it feels like it's breaking.

Maybe it's a mind that seeks clarity,
even when the fog is thick.

Maybe it's a spirit that craves the presence
 of something bigger than the self.

Maybe it's an unseen force,
a reminder you aren't alone,
no matter how many others
say grace at your table.

THAT BLUE LIGHT

There's a time,
as each day's light
fades to nothing,
when the sky, framed
by black silhouetted trees,
holds the kind of blue
that reminds you
how the depths
of the sea look
on a clear day.

It's the time that
asks you to wonder
about life: Should
you be doing this
or starting that?
Planning that
or exploring this?
The list can be long
when that blue light
comes to call.

But it feels good
to wonder and dream,
when wondering and dreaming
are underlaid by a strong
foundation of gratitude
for what already is.

SOMETIMES

Sometimes wildflowers
fill highway ditches and
the scent of pine on a hot day
in August filters through
sticky air to remind me that
I am here, now, and
that is a very good thing.

Sometimes I can see clearly
into the eyes of peace,
into the churning energy
that glues together life on earth,
like a long ago memory
of weeping willows brushing
texture on still waters.

Sometimes I move beyond
the broken tea cups and
crushed blossoms
deep into the solace
that exists in each moment—
into the grace of life
that touches everything.

SOME NOTES ON BEING ALIVE

When you pay attention to
how things grow, and
really notice what you see
no matter how hard it is
not to look away; when you
listen to what you hear
no matter how sad the story,
always feeling deep in your bones
what you know you need to feel,
you discover the sort of stuff
that allows a person
to be fully alive and
wholly present
in this strange
yet exquisite
dance of life.

CEDAR TREE SENTINEL

She stands, rooted,
surrounded by undulation,
yet rises strong even
as seasons change
as cultures dictate
as energy churns
as light and dark
seek solace in each other, and
demons and angels
trade places in jest.
Still she stands
rooted in something
beyond light and dark
beyond demon and angel
buried deep in the bedrock
of what may always
remain unseen.

COMING TO OUR SENSES

Maybe we need
to be cured by

a rainstorm's earthy flavor
a wildflower's intoxicating scent
the view of stars at night
a misty morning fog tickling naked skin
the echo of a hawk's piercing cry.

Maybe we need
to come to our senses
and wake up
to the beauty of the world
that lives more fully
when we notice all the parts.

ENCHANTMENT

Be enamored
with your existence
in a way that makes
the ordinary sparkle
with the brilliance
of a thousand sunsets.

HONEY & LIGHT

Let a gentle tide of acceptance
wash over you like a golden
cascade of honey and light,

coating curve of hip, softness of belly
lines of life etched into skin:
a remembrance of miracles.

Humming a lover's lullaby -
a longing fulfilled, beautiful
wholeness finally embraced.

THE GOD I KNOW, PART THREE

The God I know
sits on the street with those
closest to fear as pain and grief collide.

The God I know
wonders when we will figure out
what it truly means to love one another.

The God I know
reminds us that thoughts
and prayers alone aren't enough.

The God I know
calls for right action, the sort that
opens hearts and minds in new ways.

The God I know
points to a bridge, one with
the capacity to carry heavy loads.

The God I know
walks across the bridge
to offer peace to a stranger.

The God I know
whispers continually that not
all is lost even when we think it is.

COMMUNION

COMMUNING WITH THE COSMOS

Isn't it astonishing? That a
broken Cottonwood branch
can remind you that you are earth,
you are stars, you are ether—part of the
pulse that rumbles deep in the universe, to
be picked up by anyone who might take
notice they hold a fist full of stars.

HOW TO WORK

Pretend there's a string
attached to your head,
pulling toward the ceiling.

Roll your shoulders back.
Enjoy the crunching sound
your shoulder blades make
after a morning of hunching forward.

Go outside for a few minutes
if you can spare the time,
perhaps even keeping
company with birds
and trees and other wild things.

Take a long breath
deep into your abdomen,
hold it for three seconds
and breathe out.

Repeat as often as necessary.

When you feel out of tune,
check in with your physical body,
and the body of the earth.

Feel the air going in and out of your nose.
Remember you are a living,
breathing human animal.

TEA

In the evening
(or anytime, really)
take a kettle
and fill it with water.

Put it on the stove,
and let the heat
invite steam to sing.

Pour the water
over dried herbs—
loose leaf, or in a bag.

Let it sit,
and sit with it.
Maybe outside.

After 5 minutes, or ten,
have passed,
breathe the steeping scent

as you close your eyes
to remember
what it feels like
to love
yourself
enough
to notice
every drop.

BREAD

Mix flour, water, yeast
perhaps some honey and oil.
Knead until the kinks of the day
soften into something smoother,

edges not so rough.

Set it to rest somewhere warm,
and when things have expanded enough,
punch it down to create a new shape.
Let it rest again, in that warm place.

Take an hour to expand along with it.

Marvel at the way simple things
come together to form nourishment,
comfort,
and peace.

Let the alchemy
of actions taken
mold you, too,
into something new.

RESERVATIONS

Go out
even if the skies
threaten to weep,
because weeping skies
paint the ground
with a muted splendor,
one that's reserved
for days you'd
rather stay in.

SUPERIOR

I picked up a stone
the other day
on a rocky beach,
and all at once
I was a part
of something
bigger than myself;
something sacred.

How does the earth
always know how
to remind me
I am made
of the same stuff
as stars
        water
            rocks
and all the other things
that quietly make me whole?

BAPTIZE

Walk to the shore and
stare into the cool,
murky depths.
Wonder what life lies
beneath the surface and
imagine what it might
be like to look through
a different lens
at the world.

Dip one toe, and then
a foot and finally
let go to fall forward
into a baptism of gasps
that ignite your blood and
invite you to move
through the rest of the day
fully refreshed, renewed,
and awake.

CURIOSITY

Get up with the sun and
wander outside, maybe to
pick a handful of wild raspberries
or watch a drop of dew roll lazily
down a piece of slender grass
glistening in virgin morning light.

Wonder what the day could bring,
but don't think about it too long—
just enough to invite
the sort of curiosity
that makes a person
glad to be breathing.

SUNFLOWER

I tried to grow
ten foot sunflowers
for six years
before, one year,
some confident seeds
poked sprouts
through ebony soil
and stretched toward
their namesake.

That year they seemed
to grow six inches a day,
until their radiant faces
towered over me, declaring
themselves tall enough.

That year the sun rejoiced
as the blossoms wept
in gratitude
for the chance to feel
what it can be like
to embody your full
and glorious potential.

TRANSPORTATION

I turn the stone, the one
with holes dotting every curve,
over in my hand, feeling
the bumps and grooves
a life spent at sea created.

As I stand on
the basement floor,
I can feel the breeze
that swept along
the rocky coastline.

The taste of salt is in the air,
the sort that lingers
at the water's edge, and
a sense of connection
washes over me
like a wave.

I am transported
to a place
across the world,

and all at once I
I am stone,
coast,

and sea,
even while I am
body,
mind,
and spirit.

WILD AIR AND FADING STARLIGHT

Greet the new day
grounded in reality:
Walk outside to see
tired stars fade into dawn.

Touch unexpectedly soft moss
on the north sides of trees.
Be curious about the ways life
finds to express itself.

Breathe the scent of freedom
that rides with redwing blackbirds
and snow geese, remembering
truth always finds a way home.

Revel in mornings
full of wild air and
fading starlight.

KNOWLEDGE

I can't tell you much about
the latest trends in fashion,
or phones or apps or cars,
or the what the best
show is on Netflix,
but I can tell you where
to find blackberry brambles
that tower three feet over your head,
or what a well-trodden deer path looks like,
the ones they like to meander as dusk
falls in stillness over the lake, and
how the sound of a loon's cry
still pierces the darkness
even after all this time.

CANOE

We slip the big green canoe
clumsily into the lake, and
push off the dock into open water.

You hold the sides,
sitting tall on the floor,
anxious we might tip and
go for an unintended swim.

I paddle slowly, one stroke at a time;

Dip, pull, glide.

Again.

Dip, pull, glide.

Hurrying doesn't work right now.

As we round the final curve,
the afternoon sun shines
through budded trees,
emerging like those last left
by the brush of the Painter.

We applaud in silent awe
at how something as simple
as the alignment of
water
trees
light
creates a masterpiece
every single day,
just by existing.

MONARCH

Stand close to the flowers—marvel—
at what it's like to share space
with creatures who experience life

by making friends with wind,
dancing on sunbeams, and
tasting late summer's nectar by

declaring a small slice
of one half forgotten garden
a good place to exist for a little while.

Let them remind you that
sunbeams, freedom, and a bit of nectar
are needs shared by all creatures

whether those creatures
walk, fly or text
into life's next moment.

DUSK

It gives itself to every day,
this promise of night,
as light slips away like silk,
leaving softness to
settle over the landscape.

Frogs sing and blackbirds trill,
beaver finishes a day's work, and
a solitary loon wails to find his mate, while
three geese indulge in one more conversation
as the wood duck glides silently toward shore.

There are, of course,
still things to do.
Yet for many it is time to rest, so
the forest listens because
wildness generally knows what's best.

Tomorrow will come
as the sun rises in the east,
another chance to embrace a day,
but now—now it is time to soften.
Give in to the coming of the night.

RIPENING

When the berries turn black
you know the time for growth
is nearing its resting place,
and though we tend to think
growth is always desirable,
ripening shows us
it's just one part of the story.
Because, after all,
a berry that tries to grow forever
loses its sweetness and
falls to the ground.

NIGHT WOODS

It is important
every now and then
to step over roots
and around branches,
not always seeing clearly
what lies ahead,
letting your hands
and the soles of your feet
find a way forward,
as night woods,
barred owl,
crickets,
the stillness of the air
remind you there is much more
to sight than meets the eye.

DRAGONFLY

I watched a dragonfly, today,
perched
on the tip of a young asparagus spear.

Poised,
waiting for just the right moment
to burst into the next,

translucent wings
sparkling
in warm afternoon air.

For that moment
we were just two creatures
locked in tandem—

All at once different, yet
part of the same universal whole;
the great web of all that exists.

As the next moment
became the present, I
glanced toward the breeze, and

the dragonfly vanished,
as insect and atmosphere and human
stepped as one toward time itself.

BEFORE THE STORM

When things start shifting,
and the air can't decide between
damp or dry or cool or warm, you
know it's time for something to
happen, perhaps something
magical. Because conditions
are just right to coax
holding on and letting go
into cooperation,
transforming the air
with an energy
that knows how to
converse with stars
and dance with seeds
that have yet to disperse
in a cloud of wonder.

AFTER THE STORM

And then came
calm and sun
as wonder
overtook
the earth.

THE CARESS OF THE DARK

If there's a full moon
it's a time of luminescence
shimmering on the lake,
dancing with the spirits
who come out to play
in such conditions.

If the moon is hiding
behind persistent clouds
making everything black as coal,
it's a time of listening as
sight becomes less important
than feeling a way forward.

No matter how the moon looks
nor how thick the air with night,
it's a time to experience
what is possible when spirit,
 listening
and shadow
commune,
making the earth shiver with anticipation
under the caress of the dark.

TRANSITIONAL LIGHT

Spend some time
with beings
who buzz around
from weed to weed
finding the treasures
that exist even in the unwanted,
the un-orderly,
the chaotic.
Because when you
follow that lead,
well.
All sorts of hidden pathways
become illuminated
by unexpected light,
welcoming your curiosity
with the sort of enthusiasm
that perhaps, one day,
you can respond to with joy.

LAKE

You are born each spring
as the ice acquiesces to the sun.
For weeks, maybe a month
you are as smooth and
pure as new skin.

Adolescence starts in June
when the lily pads start
experimenting with independence, and
suddenly you bloom into fullness
as the reeds tower along your shores
for a time of glory.

In autumn, you start to surrender
to cooling conditions, and
age slows you into softening, reflection,
as preparations for the stillness
of winter take priority.

Then one day it comes with the frost,
all at once your wisdom becoming
something else entirely,
until it is time, again,
to be born anew.

UNNAMEABLE PRESENCE

It's been said that God
is raindrops on yellow leaves
that have fallen to the ground;
beginnings and endings, even
large stretches of seemingly
unremarkable time;
hot tea and the love that
goes into making a cup
for someone else;
the way uncertainty waltzes
with deep knowing; how
contrast contains the
beauty of shadow.
Somehow all these
names are woven
together into a
presence that is
sometimes
referred to
as God.

THE GOD I KNOW, PART FOUR

The God I know
is Rizpah on the mountain
seeking justice for her boys.

The God I know
sees color in a way that
honors stories of the other.

The God I know
calls us all into figuring out
what it means to be a good neighbor.

The God I know
isn't afraid to show up
in inconvenient places.

The God I know
remains, even amidst
uncertainty, confusion and heartache.

The God I know
is clear that while we may be one human race,
the color white has wielded too much power for too long.

The God I know
moves to crack and crumble privilege
into something that looks more like love.

BENEDICTION

PASSION

Sometimes flowers
look more like flames,
reminding us that we too
can disrupt the usual
with unexpected fire.

WHAT THE SKY KNOWS

Believe the sky
when it shows you
how to weep so
mountains rise up,
inviting joy to spring
from the depths of sorrow.

ONENESS

We could say
you are God, and
so am I, along with
that barn owl and the field
of yellow flowers and those two
crows, the ones sitting atop a
huge blue spruce, peering
down, seeming to know
much more than I do
about the ways of
the universe.

WHAT COMES NEXT

What comes next?
We can't know.

All we can do
is keep living forward,

Through the moments that we have,
letting uncertainty ride shotgun.

Because companions shrouded
in mystery keep things lively.

Just don't let uncertainty drive
if it only answers to the name fear.

SHIFTING CURRENTS

Autumn days are
good for witnessing
wind summon the
kind of change
you don't much want,
but the kind of change
you might just need.

Transition is blustery, always
shifting things around
before you're ready
to gather all that stuff
you thought you needed.
Turns out shifting currents
know the way to go, after all.

COME OF AGE

"Look, we don't fall
like flowers,
with only one season
behind us," wrote Rilke,
and when it comes
to the forest,
we can see this
is true every time
we walk through age
and celebrate the way
leaves and reflection and
the passing of time
make us feel more alive
than we thought we could feel.

UNACKNOWLEDGED GLORY

The earth still
comes alive in
jackets of gold
even if the rain
doesn't stop
to applaud.

BE IN THE CONVERSATION, NOT THE FIGHT

The flowers held on
despite being knocked
down and tied back up again,

played host to
flocks of monarchs in transit,
swarms of feasting honey bees,

hues that seemed to shout,
"Look, I'm wonderful
just by existing."

They persisted in holding heads high
even as neighbors dropped, one by one,
deeper into the season of surrender.

Then finally, as the air collected
tiny drops of snow, the kind that
remind you of how ice sounds,

time came to listen for
beauty of another kind,
the sort that helps you enter

a conversation with winter,
instead of wishing things were different
or getting into a fight you know you can't win.

ONCE UPON A TIME

The birds were out
in full force this morning,
making sure the day knew even
in its gray, grieving state, that yes
the world was meant to be celebrated
as the ones with red wings and their voices
show us that to sing at daybreak as well as dusk
helps heal the world a little bit more through joy and
tells us that yes, somehow and somewhere, people
were birds, once upon a time, and that so often a
simple understanding, one that looks deeply
in the clear eyes of murky ponds in autumn
is what we all need so we can add our
voices to the chorus of creation and
proclaim, as Omid Safi did, that
love will have the victory at
the end of days.

REFLECTIONS ON MOVING WATER

When things seem bleak,
bright spots few and far between,
days gray and flat, such conditions
coupled with heavy conversation
about the state of the world,
can result in a lot of
sighing and melancholy, so
it's best to seek company
of moving water—a poignant reminder
despite gloom, despair, guilt, and uncertainty,
the energy of the world remains fluid.
Try as we might to let stagnancy rhein,
such ways of thinking don't have
enough power to stick around
when we actively seek truth.

SKIING AROUND THE LAKE ON A WEDNESDAY

Then, as you are lamenting
all that is wrong in the world;

everything that needs fixing
seeming too vast for real change,

a fox bursts out of the woods, running
full tilt across the expanse of frozen white;

a blur of red wildness reminding you
moments like this have the power to

counter the bleak, to remind you
how simple joy can be, to shore up your

foundation just enough to keep working
toward what must be done to contribute

to the healing of the world, a more beautiful world
our hearts know is possible.

WHAT JOY IS, PART TWO

Joy is waking up to
piles of freshly fallen snow
a day you don't have to drive anywhere.

Joy is walking in the door after
skiing around a frozen lake in biting wind
toward a wood stove's warm glow.

Joy is discovering your phone died, then
realizing your woodland trek
will be better without it.

Joy is looking out the window
just in time to see sun's masterpiece
splashed across the westerly sky.

Joy is taking enough moments to
slow down and savor all that reminds you
what being alive is supposed to feel like.

UNANTICIPATED DELIGHT

With winter comes darkness,
yet somehow promises of light whisper
through inky black, long nights.

There is snow and cold alongside
moments of inspiration bursting
through gloom by way of errant sunbeams.

There is monochrome for miles,
and one bright red wool scarf
worn by a whistling wanderer.

There is glare ice and cursing on highways
singing hymns with a thousand twinkling stars
humming harmonies with their sister, moon.

There is joy,
there is sadness
existing side by side.

What I want in life
is an aptitude for astonishment,
room for unanticipated delight.

A DANCE OF MOSS AND PINE

There is
in all things
a wholeness
that remains hidden
until we stop to look at
the layers that make up this
strange human experience,
this sacred dance of
shadow and light,
moss and pine,
lament and
jubilee.

WINTER SOLSTICE

Darkness is deep and
wide, snuggled up close to
these days of winter solstice.
The vastness of night drapes a
heavy arm over Earth's northern hip
inviting us to nestle into the dark, yet
even on the days when light feels
like nothing but a wispy memory,
promise of its return can soften
blackness to velvet, inviting
our faces to turn east,
where each morning,
the sun reminds us:
with the darkest
moment comes
a restoration
of the light.

ROOT AND RISE

There will be a day—
in spring, or maybe summer—
(could be anytime, really)
when humanity rises up
rooted like a great Oak,
connected like a web of Aspen

branches intertwining,
reaching skyward
as roots tunnel deep
into the belly of the earth
intent on drinking in
    nourishment
        strength
           wisdom.

That day the people
will remember that time
when they were birds, and
lift voices in song
filling the air with
sweet
    fierce
        compassionate
          music.

Yes, there will be a day
when we all root and rise
remember and sing, and
earth will rejoice
as a collective hallelujah
blooms over the land.

AFTERWORD

AS MUCH AS I'D LIKE TO BE ABLE TO OFFER THE CURE for whatever ails anyone who comes across these words, there are no easy answers to the question of "what will it take to heal?" But that's how it is in a human life, as much as we want it to be different. We want a quick fix, the kind of 'self care' that is Instagram worthy, a pill that will make things better, the one right thing that will turn the tide in our favor. I've wanted all of those things at one time or another in the past, and I probably will again in the future. For now, though, and I hope you'll join me, I'm going to try to focus on what I can control. Focusing on what is within our power takes work, as does this thing called healing. And it's often work that looks different than you think it should. I've come to the conclusion that healing isn't something that a human eventually achieves—it's simply part of what it means to be alive on this planet. It can be mean recovering from an illness, but it can also (and so often needs to) mean finding peace outside the limitations of the physical body.

I'll be continuing to claim my story by way of the practices that work for me; by paying attention to the things that make me believe in the good of the world and by accepting my own imperfections. Healing doesn't mean striving for perfect health or the absence of disease, though those things would be nice for many of us. It means offering ourselves "simple gestures of respect," as Sharon Salzberg puts it—things like allowing the mind to rest now and then, nourishing the soul with prayer or art or dance, giving the body the gift of healthy food, reading something that brings joy, wandering in the woods on a lunch break, saying "I'll try again tomorrow."

There are many ways to practice offering gestures of respect, or love, and that's what's important to remember: That self love is a practice. There is no pass/fail – there is only the willingness to give yourself grace—again, and again, and again. Respecting yourself, scars and all, is the gateway to self love and the path toward healing. It's the way to claim the story that wants to speak through you. And that story, the one that is truly yours to embody, is the one that's going to contribute to the healing of the world at large.

Claiming your story takes patience and persistence. It takes the sort of self compassion that might, one day, paint the sky with a splendor that can only be found by falling into the fractured radiance that defines what it means to be alive on planet earth. Be brave enough to look through a different lens if you need to, and explore an unfamiliar path. Let the stumbles and the joys and everything in between lead you toward hallelujah. I'll meet you there.

ENDNOTES

"When People Were Birds" was inspired by a line by Terry Tempest Williams in *When Women Were Birds: Fifty Four Variations on Voice.*

"Communing with the Cosmos" was inspired by *A Fistful of Stars: Communing with the Cosmos* by Gail Collins-Ranadive, with Milt Hetrick.

"Unnameable Presence" was inspired by *Naming the Unnameable: 89 Wonderful and Useful Names for God* by Matthew Fox.

In "Mountain Shadow" the use of the words 'Mother Culture' (defined as a collective term for any given culture's most influencing features) was inspired by Daniel Quinn, who uses the words in his book *Ishmael.*

In "Skiing Around the Lake on a Wednesday" the last line was inspired by *The More Beautiful World Our Hearts Know is Possible,* a book by Charles Eisenstein.

In "The God I Know, Part Two" the last stanza was inspired by Glennon Doyle and the work of the organization Together Rising.

"Honey & Light" was inspired by the song "Heavenly Body" written by jazz vocalist Nancy Harms.

Acknowledgments

MANY THANKS to Lindsay Ruder, Holly Walsh, and Christina Beck for reading early drafts that seemed like jumbles of words in no particular order. Thank you to James Scott Smith for pushing me to make the final manuscript better than it would have been otherwise. Your encouragement and guidance made such a difference in the end result of the collection itself, as well as my confidence in releasing it to the world. Thanks to the Martin Lake Poetry Workshop folks, for providing feedback during the final editing phase.

Thank you to my faithful community of followers on social media—your response to my initial dabblings in poetry were what lead me to think a published collection might be a viable idea. The support of readers is so important, so thank you for yours.

And of course, thank you to my family: Dad, for sitting up with me that one night when I was visiting and I couldn't stop coughing. Mom, for always believing things will work out. Nick, for your constant love and support even when I was feeling my lowest. Eva, for being yourself, even when I wasn't feeling like myself—and for always reminding me that being present is the best option available.

About the Author

Award winning author of several books, Heidi Barr is committed to cultivating ways of being that are life-giving and sustainable for people, communities and the planet. She works as a wellness coach, holds a Master's degree in Faith and Health Ministries and occasionally partners with organic farms and yoga teachers to offer retreat experiences. At home in Minnesota, she lives with her husband and daughter where they tend a large vegetable garden, explore nature and do their best to live simply.

VISIT HER AT WWW.HEIDIBARR.COM

HOMEBOUND PUBLICATIONS

Ensuring that the mainstream isn't the only stream.

AT HOMEBOUND PUBLICATIONS, we publish books written by independent voices for independent minds. Our books focus on a return to simplicity and balance, connection to the earth and each other, and the search for meaning and authenticity. We strive to ensure that the mainstream is not the only stream. In all our titles, our intention is to introduce new perspectives that will directly aid humankind in the trials we face at present as a global village.

WWW.HOMEBOUNDPUBLICATIONS.COM
LOOK FOR OUR TITLES WHEREVER BOOKS ARE SOLD

SINCE 2011

Printed in the USA
CPSIA information can be obtained
at www.ICGtesting.com
JSHW082351140824
68134JS00020B/2014

9 781938 846854